When Mom Came Home

George R. Addison III

To order additional copies of this book, contact:
Xlibris
1-888-795-4274
www.Xlibris.com
Orders@Xlibris.com

ISBN:	Softcover	978-1-4691-7971-1
	EBook	978-1-4691-7972-8

Print information available on the last page

Rev. date: 07/25/2020

Mom was away for a long time. Grandma said that Mom got a job that took her far, far away. She says that Mom is working for all of us. She's fighting for peace in another country.

I missed Mom the most at night-time. Most nights she read me a story before I went to bed. Sometimes she made the stories up herself or she told me stuff about our family. This is how I found out that Grandpa Joe was in the Army just like Mommy. Only Grandpa Joe went to a place called Vietnumb, not I-Rock.

Grandma smiled and her face looked young, like Mama's. "That's because you are trying to remember up here," and she pointed to my head, "When you can only remember her in here," she pointed to my heart.

Ms Addison
Math Quiz
2+3=2(3)
6+2-3=
9+6-5=
2+10-8=
5+12-6=

When I'm at school, I'm so busy studying for my big exam that sometimes I forget that Mom is gone. Then I think about telling her about my day or imagine what she might fix for my lunch, and I remember that my Mom went to someplace in I-Rock.

But when I get home, I really miss Mom. Grandma cooks dinner, but it's not like Mom's. Grandma doesn't like to pour gravy all over the rice. She says that fish don't belong on pizza. And on Sundays, I have to eat beets or turnips or even . . . ugghh . . . . liver!

TNW
News
Brief:
Breaking News:
3 soldiers died In Iraq

One night I got real scared because Grandma started screaming and crying. She was watching the news and they were showing dead bodies in boxes with flags on them. "They're all dead!" Grandma screamed, "They're all dead!" Grandma didn't sleep well that night. "I want my baby to come home," she whispered before she fell asleep.

The next day Grandma woke me up. “Let’s pray Marsalis. We’ll pray for your Mama to come home safely to us. May the Lord watch and protect her.” When I closed my eyes and prayed for my Mom, I tried to see her face. “Why are you crying little one, your mother will be okay.” “Grandma, I can’t remember her face! Oh Grandma. I’m a bad son, I can’t remember Mama’s face!”

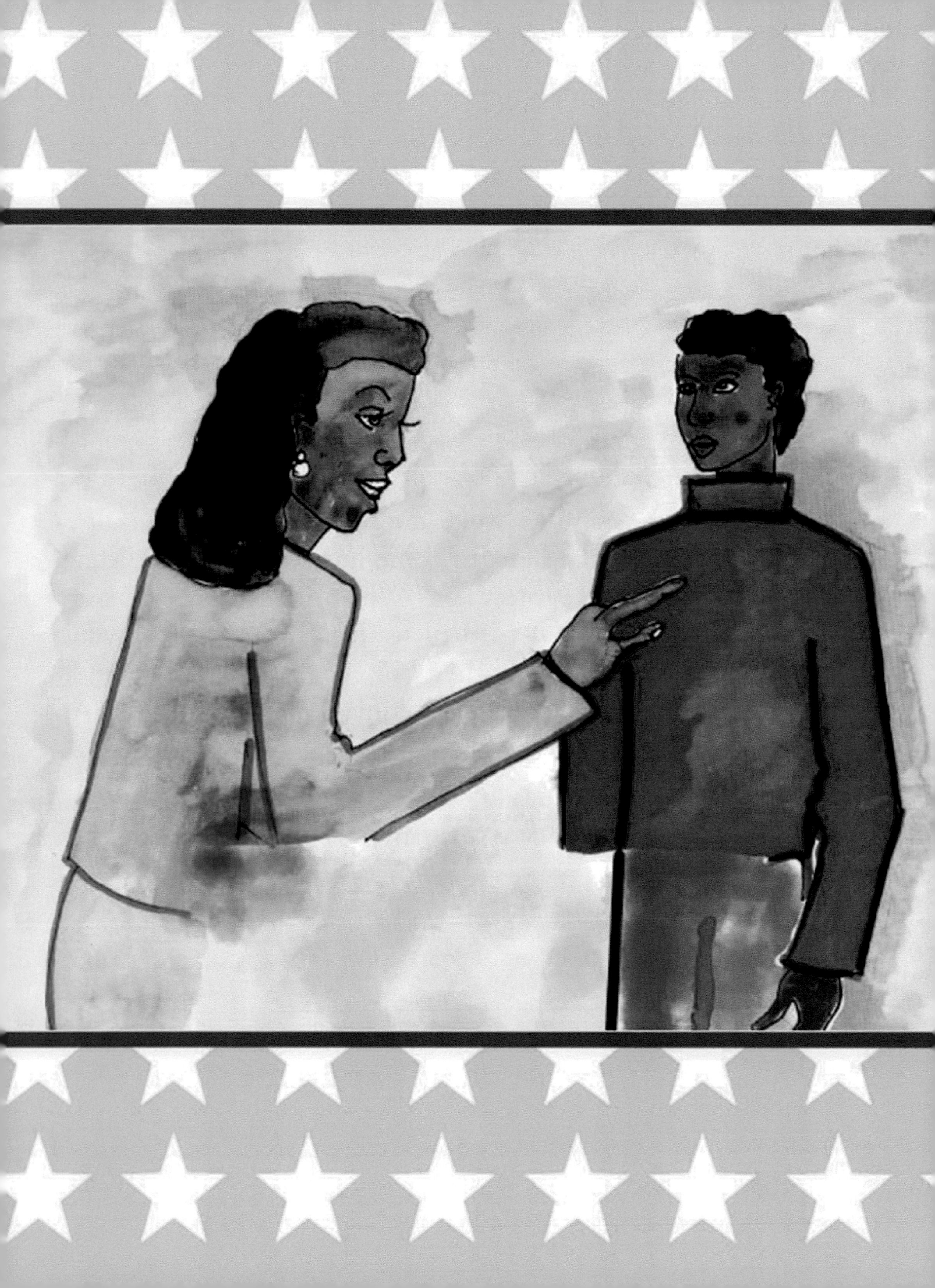

Grandma smiled and her face looked young, like Mama's. "That's because you are trying to remember up here," and she pointed to my head, "When you can only remember her in here," she pointed to my heart.

A few days later Grandma got a letter in the mail. Her face looked happy and sad at the same time. "Your Mama is finally coming home. But we still have to wait a couple of months for her to heal," she said. "From what Grandma? Did she get hurt in I-Rock?"

It still took a long time, but finally Grandma said we were going to the airport to pick up my Mom. Grandma drove a new van she bought especially for Mom.

"Yes, baby. Your mother was hurt real bad. She lost her legs. When she comes home she is gonna need your help." "How could Mama lose her legs?" Grandma told me what happened in the war. She said something called scrapple got caught in Mom's back.

When I first saw my Mom, it was kind of like a dream because she looked like my Mom but different. My Mom could walk when she left, now she was in a chair with wheels on it. Still, I jumped in her lap. I was sooo happy to see her.

I love my mom even if she is in a wheelchair. I know she used to make me lunch but now I'm learning to make sandwiches and stuff for my Mom. And Grandma says she'll teach me how to cook for Mom too!

Mom is still so cool! She plays basketball with me. And she flies kites with me. She comes to all my school plays and takes me to the movies every Saturday. Mom is still Mom. And I still love her very, very much!

Printed in the United States
By Bookmasters